Facilitator's Guide

Clifton L. Taulbert • Douglas E. Decker

Eight
Habits of
the Heart™
for Educators

**Building Strong
School Communities
Through Timeless Values**

CORWIN PRESS
A SAGE Publications Company
Thousand Oaks, CA 91320

For information:

Corwin Press
A Sage Publications Company
2455 Teller Road
Thousand Oaks, California 91320
www.corwinpress.com

Sage Publications Ltd.
1 Oliver's Yard
55 City Road
London EC1Y 1SP
United Kingdom

Sage Publications India Pvt. Ltd.
B-42, Panchsheel Enclave
Post Box 4109
New Delhi 110 017 India

Printed in the United States of America

ISBN 1–4129–5046–5 or ISBN-13 978–1–4129–5046–6

This book is printed on acid-free paper.

06   07   08   09   10   10   9   8   7   6   5   4   3   2   1

Acquisitions Editor:	Rachel Livsey
Editorial Assistant:	Phyllis Cappello
Production Editor:	Jenn Reese
Typesetter:	C&M Digitals (P) Ltd.
Proofreader:	Penny Sippel
Cover Designer:	Lisa Miller

Contents

About the Authors

**Clifton L. Taulbert** is the President and Founder of the Building Community Institute located in Tulsa, Oklahoma. Taulbert is a recognized thought leader on "Building Community" and delivers his concepts to corporate, academic, and government audiences worldwide. He was among those chosen by CNN to represent "Community" at the turn of the millennium, while his important conversation on building community is outlined in the award-winning book, *Eight Habits of the Heart,* which was named by USA TODAY as their year-end choice of books to enrich our minds and lives in 1997. As a result of a lecture on "Community" in Natchez, Mississippi, Taulbert was personally invited by Associate Supreme Court Justice, Sandra Day O'Connor, to address members of the court and their guests. Jonathan Kozol says about this book, "It moves with grace between the races." Michael Medved, nationally known talk show host has called his voice, "a national treasure," and college basketball's own John Wooden said, "I could not put it down until I completed it all."

Taulbert was born in the Mississippi Delta and educated in the secondary school system. He draws heavily from his childhood for the books he writes and the lectures he gives from Harvard University, to NATO, to Lockheed Martin, to the University Nationale in San Jose, Costa Rica, all the way to the Executive Branch of the U.S. Government.

Taulbert has authored eleven additional books, which include the international best seller, *Once Upon a Time When We Were Colored* and the Pulitzer-nominated *The Last Train North.* His first picture book, *Little Cliff and the Porch People,* was recently chosen by Target and the Miami International Book Festival Group as their choice for their annual program, One Book, One Community. His most recent book by Corwin Press, *Eight Habits of the Heart for Educators,* is being hailed as one of the most important books ever written for educators and is already having a national impact.

He serves on the National Board of Character Education Partnership, the Board of Visitors for Claremont Graduate School, and is a Trustee for The University of Tulsa. Taulbert formerly served on the Board of Advisors for Bank One and Oklahoma Investment Forum. He currently lives in Tulsa, Oklahoma, with his wife Barbara Jackson Taulbert.

 **Douglas E. Decker**, as the Assistant to the President of the Building Community Institute, is a key member of the team. As such, he works directly with the president and the outside consultants on the design and development of all Building Community and "Eight Habits of the Heart" products for educational, corporate, and government markets.

Additionally, he oversees the design and development of the customized Leadership, Diversity, Team Building, and Community Building workshops that are requested from clients and prospects throughout the country, while also serving as the coordinator of all statewide programs, including trainer certification.

Decker has the direct responsibility for the design and delivery of all the "Eight Habits of the Heart" Leadership and Diversity workshops offered by the Institute, as well as those offered to high school youth and college students.

He is an honors graduate of Oral Roberts University, an avid sportsman, and shares his life with his wife, Linzie, and their two dogs.

Introduction

This Facilitator's Guide is a companion for *Eight Habits of the Heart for Educators* by Clifton L. Taulbert. It is designed to accompany the study of the book and provide assistance to group facilitators, such as school leaders, professional development coordinators, peer coaches, team leaders, mentors, and professors. Along with a summary of each chapter in the book, Clifton L. Taulbert and Douglas E. Decker have provided chapter discussion questions, learning activities, journal writing prompts, suggestions for practical application, and resources for sustaining the learning.

When using the guide during independent study, focus on the summaries, discussion questions and practical application.

For small study groups, the facilitator should guide the group through the chapter work.

For small or large group workshops, the facilitator should create an agenda by selecting activities and discussion starters from the chapter summaries that meet the group's goals, and guide the group through the learning process.

Additional Resources for Facilitators

Corwin Press also offers a free 16-page resource entitled *Tips for Facilitators*, which includes practical strategies and tips for guiding a successful meeting. The information in this section describes different professional development opportunities, the principles of effective professional development, some characteristics of an effective facilitator, the responsibilities of the facilitator, and practical tips and strategies to make the meeting more successful. *Tips for Facilitators* is available for free download at the Corwin Press Web site (www.corwinpress.com, under "Extras").

We recommend that facilitators download a copy of *Tips for Facilitators* and review the characteristics and responsibilities of facilitators and professional development strategies for different types of work groups and settings.

Chapter-by-Chapter Study Guide

Eight Habits of the Heart for Educators

by Clifton L. Taulbert

Chapter 1. Building Community . . . The Foundation for Excellence

Summary

The premise of building community for educators and students, to obtain the goals of academic initiatives set forth, is welcomed at all levels. However, many have left themselves out of the community building process, imagined it would happen automatically, and have forgotten the importance of building community for the overall success of the student, not just the accomplishment of the academic goals. Educators have the lead in building the type of community they would like to work in and, more important, they would like the students to be a part of, for their betterment. Community must become the foundation from which all goals and initiatives are set and our youth learn and grow out of. This chapter will look at the importance of envisioning a community where positive behavior and healthy relationships exist, not only among the faculty and staff, but among the students as well, as they see community built in front of them and incorporate it into their daily lives for lifelong success.

Discussion Questions

1. Why did you first enter into education?
2. Who do you see when you look at your students?

3. Do you believe the phrase, "Your students will do what they see you do?"
4. How do you look past the demographics of each student?
5. What does 'Building Community' mean to you?
6. Do you view 'Community' as a crucial piece of the education process?

Activity

● *Defining Your Ideal Community*

Time: 15 minutes
Materials: Handout 1:1, pen/pencil, flip chart paper, markers

Ask participant's to use Handout 1:1 and to write down ONE WORD, in the first box, that represents an IDEAL community to them. (2 minutes)

Next, have each participant share their word out loud, while you write each word down on the flip chart. (3 minutes)

Then, using the words provided from each individual, create a group-wide consensus definition starting with: Community is. . . . Have participants copy this definition into the second box on Handout 1:1. (10 minutes)

Facilitator's Note: Be sure to point out that the majority of thought was the same, as it applies to what an IDEAL Community engenders. Remind participants that this definition will travel with them to each learning session.

Journal Writing Prompts

Referring to page 7 in Clifton L. Taulbert's book, *Eight Habits of the Heart for Educators,* read the list of barriers and roadblocks. Write your thoughts on how these barriers can be circumvented or completely removed through building the type of community previously defined.

Practical Application

Before adjourning the session, ask each participant to pull out Handout 1:2, *Personal Strategies to Implement—Community,* and to write one ACTION SPECIFIC strategy they will implement within 24 hours to make the ideal definition of Community come to life, for themselves, others and most importantly their students.

Close the session by challenging participants to make Building Community a primary focus each day, not only for their benefit, but also for the benefit of their students.

Chapter 2. Building Community . . . The Human Touch

Summary

Community will always be just another word without people to bring it to life, to give it a look and a feel. Recognizing the importance of building community is the first step; the second, is to understand how that is best accomplished. This chapter will discuss the power of the "human touch" to assist in building the types of communities where everyone will feel welcomed and our students, our citizen-trustees, can thrive, while providing insight into what actions can create the ideal community that everyone wants to be a part of.

Discussion Questions

1. What was the response to your strategy implementation?
2. Is it important to make Building Community personal?
3. Can you build Community when you are by yourself?
4. Is it important to think of the student when you are building Community?

Activity

● *Remembering the "Human Touch"*

Time: 25 minutes
Materials: Eight Habits of the Heart postcards, pen/pencil, tissue, *Eight Habits of the Heart for Educators* by Clifton L. Taulbert

Have participants recall their school days and think of one person that they remember who provided them the important community-building "Human Touch." (2 minutes)

Next, have each participant write a thank you postcard to that person for that specific act that they remember and how it has impacted their life. (8 minutes)

Ask four or five volunteers to share their postcards with the entire learning group. (15 minutes)

Facilitator's Note: This is a powerful activity that drives home the importance of the "Human Touch" in the lives of students today. Be mindful of the participant's reaction to this activity and be prepared for some tearful memories. Encourage each participant to send this thank you postcard on to the recipient if they are still alive today.

Journal Writing Prompts

PART 1: Make a list of the top five most influential people in your lives to the present day. Next to their names write the unselfish act that they performed toward you that placed them on your list.

PART 2: Now list three people that you would like to positively impact through the "Human Touch."

Practical Application

Have participants pull out Handout 2:1, *Personal Strategies to Implement—Human Touch,* and write one ACTION SPECIFIC strategy they will direct toward each of the three individuals listed in PART 2 of the Journal Prompts, to extend the "Human Touch" and begin building community.

Close the session by challenging participants to make Building Community a primary focus each day for the success of their students.

Chapter 3. Building Community . . . Life Lessons From the Mississippi Delta

Summary

Community will always include others and will always benefit from individual Intentional Unselfishness. In this chapter, Taulbert recalls the first time he truly realized that the People surrounding him as a child were what brought Community to the table, through their daily unselfish acts. The Eight Habits of the Heart, unselfish acts brought to life by the "Porch People" of the Mississippi Delta . . . the look and feel of the "Human Touch," are introduced and you will see how these Habits can positively impact your life and the lives of your students by forming a strong foundation of Community throughout your school. The Eight Habits of the Heart are:

Nurturing Attitude	Brotherhood
Responsibility	High Expectations
Dependability	Courage
Friendship	Hope

Discussion Questions

1. Did you include students in Part 2 of your list?
2. In today's society, do you think it is proper for staff, parents and community members to all play a part in the students' education?

3. Who do you see when you think of these Eight Habits of the Heart?
4. Do your students see these Habits on a daily basis?

Activity

● *Pre-Assessment Benchmark*

Time: 10 minutes
Materials: Clifton L. Taulbert's Benchmark Chart (Handout 3:1), multicolored pens/pencils, *Eight Habits of the Heart for Educators* by Clifton L. Taulbert

Introduce Clifton L. Taulbert's Benchmark Chart on page 122 in *Eight Habits of the Heart for Educators*, by Clifton L. Taulbert, by reading to the second full paragraph on page 121. (2 minutes)
Next, have each participant refer to the definitions of the Eight Habits of the Heart on page 27 of *Eight Habits of the Heart for Educators* by Clifton L. Taulbert and honestly assess where they believe they are, at present, on the chart, in a single color. (8 minutes)
Facilitator's Note: The Benchmark Chart will be used after each remaining chapter for review and re-assessment of participant's position. Be sure to remind participants to bring the Benchmark Chart to each learning session.

Journal Writing Prompts

Reflecting on the definitions of the Eight Habits of the Heart, write down how each of these Habits can help you reach your ultimate goal of your Ideal Community.

Practical Application

Have participants begin to build each of the Eight Habits of the Heart into their daily lives and the lives of their students by performing the four Opportunities to Bring the Human Touch to Your School on page 29 of *Eight Habits of the Heart for Educators* by Clifton L. Taulbert.
Close the session by challenging participants to make Building Community a primary focus each day for the success their students.

Chapter 4. Nurturing Attitude: The First Habit of the Heart

Summary

As our master plan is to build a Community conducive to an excellent learning environment for our youth . . . our citizen-trustees, we must have the necessary tools to be able to build such a Community. The first of these tools is Nurturing Attitude. Within our schools a Nurturing Attitude is characterized by unselfish caring, supportiveness and a willingness to share time.

Discussion Questions

1. What role does Nurturing Attitude play in your daily routines at present?
2. What are a few underlying traits of Nurturing Attitude?
3. Would you rearrange your schedule to be the answer for a new teacher or a student who without you would not be able to move forward?
4. How can Nurturing Attitude assist you in your position?

Activities

● *Understanding Nurturing Attitude*

Time: 20 minutes
Materials: Handout 4:1 (Nurturing Attitude Activity and Notes sheet), pen/pencil, *Eight Habits of the Heart for Educators* by Clifton L. Taulbert

Have a participant read From the Front Porch on page 38 of Clifton L. Taulbert's *Eight Habits of the Heart for Educators*. While it is being read, ask participants to mentally identify the deed(s) or act(s) in the passage that look like Nurturing Attitude. (5 minutes)

Next, have participants partner up and discuss how this Habit of the Heart LOOKS in their classroom, their hallways and their school. From this discussion, have them each select one powerful characteristic that sticks out to them that they did not originally think of. Have them share their choices out loud with the group. (15 minutes)

Facilitator's Note: Chart common traits/characteristics, to provide common thoughts and ideas on Nurturing Attitude. Remind participants that a Nurturing Attitude may be represented by different people, but it looks the same everywhere.

● *Benchmarking Nurturing Attitude*

Time: 1 minute
Materials: Handout 3:1 (Clifton L. Taulbert's Benchmark Chart), multicolored pens/pencils

Have participant's get out the Benchmark Chart (Handout 3:1) and, using a different-color writing utensil than before, re-assess their position within Nurturing Attitude after today's learning session and place their new position on the chart.

Journal Writing Prompts

PART 1: Reflecting on the reading from Clifton L. Taulbert's book *Eight Habits of the Heart for Educators*, what does "Slowing Your Pace" look like?

PART 2: What would happen to your school community should students; parents and educators adopt this type of Community?

Practical Application

Have participants pull out Handout 4:2, *Personal Strategies to Implement—Nurturing Attitude*, and write one ACTION SPECIFIC strategy in the top box; they will direct toward a student within 24 hours that will build Nurturing Attitude into their lives.

Close the session by challenging participants to step out of their comfort zone, slow down and build Nurturing Attitude among their peers, neighbors and most of all students, on a daily basis.

Chapter 5. Responsibility: The Second Habit of the Heart

Summary

Upon learning and implementing a Nurturing Attitude into our lives, we are better able to show up and lend a personal commitment to each and every task. In this chapter we will look at the second Habit of the Heart, Responsibility, and what "showing up" looks like and how it plays a role in our daily activities and interaction with peers, parents and students. Within our schools, Responsibility is showing and encouraging a personal commitment to each task.

Discussion Questions

1. Do you believe Community can be built without Responsibility?
2. What are some underlying characteristics of Responsibility?
3. How can you pass Responsibility along?

Activities

● *Understanding Responsibility*

Time: 25 minutes
Materials: Handout 5:1 (Responsibility Activity and Notes Sheet), pen/pencil, *Eight Habits of the Heart for Educators* by Clifton L. Taulbert

Have a participant read From the Front Porch on page 49 and 51 of Clifton L. Taulbert's *Eight Habits of the Heart for Educators*. While it is being read, ask participants to write down the name of one person from their education years that lived out Responsibility in front of them. Then have them write down next to the name, one action that representative performed that was Responsibility to them. (8 minutes)

Next, have participants pair up, with someone other than the partner from the Nurturing Attitude discussion, and discuss their Responsibility, the action that brought it to life and the impact that action had on their life. Be sure they take notes on each other's representative and action. From this discussion, have a few partners volunteer to share each other's choices out loud with the group and the acts that made the Responsibility. (17 minutes)

Facilitator's Note: Chart common traits/characteristics, to provide common thoughts and ideas on Responsibility. Remind participants that Responsibility may be represented by different people, but it looks the same no matter who you are or where you live.

● *Benchmarking Responsibility*

Time: 1 minute
Materials: Handout 3:1 (Clifton L. Taulbert's Benchmark Chart), multicolored pens/pencils

Have participants get out the Benchmark Chart (Handout 3:1) and, using a different-color writing utensil than before, re-assess their position within Responsibility after today's learning session and place their new position on the chart.

Journal Writing Prompts

PART 1: Reflecting on the reading from Clifton L. Taulbert's book, *Eight Habits of the Heart for Educators,* what does "Showing Up" look like?

PART 2: What would happen to your school community should students, parents, and educators bring Responsibility to the table?

Practical Application

Have participants pull out Handout 5:2, *Personal Strategies to Implement—Responsibility,* and write one ACTION SPECIFIC strategy, in the top box; they will direct toward a student within 24 hours, that will bring Responsibility to life for them.

Close the session by challenging participants to build Responsibility among their peers, neighbors and most of all students, on a daily basis. A perfect way to do so would be to implement the boxed activity on page 53 of Clifton L. Taulbert's *Eight Habits of the Heart for Educators.*

Chapter 6. Dependability: The Third Habit of the Heart

Summary

Just as Nurturing Attitude and Responsibility are pertinent to a climate where student success results, so is Dependability: being there for others through all the time of their lives, a steady influence that makes tomorrow a welcome event. In this chapter we will look at Dependability, the third Habit of the Heart and just what it means to be committed and to understand the importance of this commitment to others. We will explore what Dependability looks like and understand that this Habit of the Heart is not just mere thought or expression but strategic actions performed on a daily basis.

Discussion Questions

1. How does Dependability currently look in your life?
2. Name some character traits of Dependability?
3. Is Dependability a Habit that can be passed along? How?

Activities

● *Understanding Dependability*

Time: 25 minutes
Materials: Handout 6:1 (Dependability Activity and Notes Sheet), pen/pencil, flip chart paper, markers, *Eight Habits of the Heart for Educators* by Clifton L. Taulbert

PART A-1: Have one participant from each small group meet with other selected individuals in a separate meeting place. They should discuss how this Habit of the Heart SHOULD LOOK within the school community, based on the definition of Dependability and their reading. Be sure to have them take notes that they can bring back to their learning stations.
PART A-2: At the same time, have the remaining group members discuss how this Habit of the Heart CURRENTLY LOOKS within their school environment. Have them take notes to share with others. (13 minutes)
PART B: Have the individuals selected, return to their small learning groups and lead a discussion on the differences between the two conversations. Call for one or two volunteers to share the differences and/or similarities of Dependability among their school environments. (12 minutes)

● *Benchmarking Dependability*

Time: 1 minute
Materials: Handout 3:1 (Clifton L. Taulbert's Benchmark Chart), multicolored pens/pencils

Have participants get out the Benchmark Chart (Handout 3:1) and using a different color writing utensil than their pre-assessment, re-assess their position within Dependability after today's learning session and place their new position on the chart.

Journal Writing Prompts

PART 1: After reading the From the Front Porch in Chapter Six: Dependability, in Clifton Taulbert's text, *Eight Habits of the Heart for Educators,* how can you "flip on the lights for the students in your school and the educators with whom you serve?"

PART 2: What would happen to your school community should administration, educators and staff "put the interests of others before their own?"

Practical Application

Have participants pull out Handout 6:2, *Personal Strategies to Implement—Dependability,* and write one ACTION SPECIFIC strategy, in the top box; they will direct toward a student and one toward a parent, within 24 hours, that will bring Dependability to life.

Close the session by challenging participants to build Dependability among their peers, neighbors and most of all students, on a daily basis. Some great options to start building Dependability can be found on pages 60 and 61 of Clifton L. Taulbert's *Eight Habits of the Hear for Educators,* under Opportunity to Promote Dependability in Your School.

Chapter 7. Friendship: The Fourth Habit of the Heart

Summary

Friendship is the habit of the heart that binds people together when they take pleasure in each other's company, listen, laugh, and share good times and bad. Friendship extends a welcome, it anticipates others and most importantly, it undergirds all positive relationships. In this chapter, we discover the power of the fourth "R," Relationships . . . Friendship. We look at what it means to be a friend from an educator's perspective toward: other educators, parents/care-givers and students. After all, students will do what they see you do and, when you reach out to establish these relationships, they will respond accordingly.

Discussion Questions

1. Do you believe that positive relationships can impact learning?
2. Finish this sentence; Friendship is . . . .
3. Can Friendship exist at all levels: educator to administration, educator to parent, educator-to-educator, and educator to student? Should it exist at all levels?

Activities

● *Understanding Friendship*

Time: 25 minutes
Materials: Handout 7:1—Friendship Activity and Notes Sheet, Handout 7:2—"Blind Berta" excerpt from Clifton L. Taulbert's *Eight Habits of the Heart for Educators*

PART 1: Call for a volunteer to read aloud the "Blind Berta" excerpt (Handout 7:2), with participants listening intently. (3 minutes)
PART 2: From the reading, have participants answer the following three questions on Handout 7:1 (4 minutes per response)
1. How can "Blind Berta" impact embracing students who may be different from others?
2. How can this story impact parents/care-givers who may not understand the educational system and what it means?
3. How can this story impact educator behavior?
PART 3: Call for a few volunteers to share their responses with the learning group and lead a discussion with the entire learning group on those shared responses, directed toward ESTABLISHING POSITIVE RELATIONSHIPS FOR THE BENEFIT OF OUR YOUTH. (10 minutes)

● *Benchmarking Friendship*

Time: 1 minute
Materials: Handout 3:1 (Clifton L. Taulbert's Benchmark Chart), multicolored pens/pencils

Have participants get out the Benchmark Chart (Handout 3:1) and, using a different-color writing utensil than their pre-assessment, re-assess their position within Friendship after today's learning session and place their new position on the chart.

Journal Writing Prompts

Write down your thoughts on what it means to "anticipate the needs of others" and how you may be able to do this better, on a daily basis.

Practical Application

Have participants pull out Handout 7:3, *Personal Strategies to Implement—Friendship,* and write one ACTION SPECIFIC strategy, in the top box; they will direct toward a student and one toward a fellow educator in the presence of students, within 24 hours, that will bring Friendship to life.

Close the session by challenging participants to build Friendship among their peers, neighbors and most of all students, on a daily basis. Some great options to start building Friendship can be found on page 71 of Clifton L. Taulbert's *Eight Habits of the Heart for Educators,* under Opportunity to Promote Friendship in Your School.

Chapter 8. Brotherhood: The Fifth Habit of the Heart

Summary

Today, our society's population and demographics are changing more than ever. Just look into the classrooms and schools within your community. However, with this great change comes great opportunity. To ensure exceptional learning and personal growth, educators must lead the way in creating school environments where everyone is respected, affirmed and included. When you respect, affirm and include others, you are setting a personal example for your students and allowing them to recognize the importance of reaching beyond comfortable. In this chapter we will explore Brotherhood, the Fifth Habit of the Heart, the habit that reaches beyond comfortable relationships to extend a welcome to those who may be different from ourselves.

Discussion Questions

1. Where did you first see Brotherhood lived out in front of you?
2. Are there barriers to "reaching beyond comfortable"?
3. What do you think will happen if you do "reach beyond comfortable"?

Activities

- *Understanding Brotherhood*

Time: 20 minutes
Materials: Handout 8:1—Brotherhood Activity and Notes Sheet, large flip chart paper, colored markers, scotch tape

PART 1: Have the learning group break into small groups of four to five participants. (Aim for at least four small groups.) Give each small group a piece of large flip chart paper and markers. Ask half of the small groups to draw a picture of a school/learning environment WITHOUT Brotherhood. Ask the other half of the small groups to draw a picture of a school/learning environment WITH Brotherhood. Be sure to make them aware that they will share their drawings. (12 minutes)

PART 2: Have each small group in its entirety, starting with the groups that were WITHOUT Brotherhood, come up to the front of the room and share their drawing, and why they chose to draw their perspective that way. Have them hang up the pictures on the wall for everyone to see at the remaining meetings as a reminder of the importance to build community. (8 minutes)

- *Benchmarking Brotherhood*

Time: 1 minute
Materials: Handout 3:1 (Clifton L. Taulbert's Benchmark Chart), multicolored pens/pencils

Have participants get out the Benchmark Chart (Handout 3:1) and, using a different-color writing utensil than their pre-assessment, re-assess their position within Brotherhood after today's learning session and place their new position on the chart.

Journal Writing Prompts

Write down every act of Reaching Beyond Comfortable that you see for one week, while also making note of the responses. How did this act make the beneficiary feel? Was the reach beyond comfortable worth it?

Practical Application

Have participants pull out Handout 8:2, *Personal Strategies to Implement—Brotherhood,* and write one ACTION SPECIFIC strategy, in the top box, to reach beyond comfortable to someone who may be different from yourself (in the presence of students), within the next 24 hours.

Close the session by challenging participants to build Brotherhood within all the areas of their lives. Some great options to start building Brotherhood can be found on pages 82 and 83 of Clifton L. Taulbert's *Eight Habits of the Heart for Educators*, under Intentional Strategies to Promote Brotherhood and Opportunity to Promote Brotherhood in Your School.

Chapter 9. High Expectations: The Sixth Habit of the Heart

Summary

Throughout our learning, we have discussed the vision that educators must have for who students can become. This vision reflects itself in everything that you do and say to your students. The voice of validation is key to the success of each student and cannot be brought to the table without everyone being a part. In this chapter we look at High Expectations: believing that others can be successful, telling them so, and praising their accomplishments. While also discovering why it is so crucial that everyone: superintendents, staff, faculty, parents/care-givers and community leaders, all live out and become this for each and every student they encounter.

Discussion Questions

1. What difference can your POSITIVE words make in the life of students, parents and other educators?
2. Do you see value in having High Expectations on a daily basis? Why or why not?

Activities

● *Understanding High Expectations*

Time: 15 minutes
Materials: Handout 9:1—High Expectations Activity and Notes Sheet

PART 1: As the facilitator, read aloud From the Front Porch on pages 87 and 88 of Clifton L. Taulbert's *Eight Habits of the Heart for Educators.* Then ask participants to write down three people and three words that describe this habit from their growing years in school. (5 minutes)
PART 2: Call for volunteers to share their lists, people and descriptive words, and chart these words. Use the charted list as a

talking point to bring to the forefront the importance of your WORDS directed toward your students and others.

● *Benchmarking High Expectations*

Time: 1 minute
Materials: Handout 3:1 (Clifton L. Taulbert's Benchmark Chart), multicolored pens/pencils

Have participants get out the Benchmark Chart (Handout 3:1) and, using a different-color writing utensil than their pre-assessment, re-assess their position within High Expectations after today's learning session and place their new position on the chart.

Journal Writing Prompts

Please write a response: How can your position become a role model for success rather than a barrier to communication?

Practical Application

Have participants pull out Handout 9:2, *Personal Strategies to Implement—High Expectations*, and write one ACTION SPECIFIC strategy, in the top box; they will direct toward a student within 24 hours, that will bring High Expectations to life.

Close the session by challenging participants to build High Expectations among all of their students, on a daily basis. Some great options to start building High Expectations can be found on page 93 of Clifton L. Taulbert's *Eight Habits of the Heart for Educators*, under Opportunity to Promote High Expectations in Your School.

Chapter 10. Courage: The Seventh Habit of the Heart

Summary

Up to now, we have studied, discussed and embraced six Habits of the Heart, but none may be as important as the seventh, Courage. In this chapter we will review the definition of Courage and see how this Habit of the Heart can become the force multiplier to all of the others before it. Without Courage, standing up and doing the right thing, speaking out on behalf of others, and making a commitment to excellence in the face of adversity or the absence of support, Nurturing Attitude, Responsibility, Dependability, Friendship, Brotherhood and High Expectations and student success . . . may never become a reality.

Discussion Questions

1. What areas of education do you believe Courage can positively affect?
2. Is there a place for Courage in everyday education? In your classroom? In your school?
3. Have you seen Courage in your current school environment? If so, how?

Activities

● *Understanding Courage*

Time: 15 minutes
Materials: Handout 10:1—Courage Activity and Notes Sheet, Clifton L. Taulbert's *Eight Habits of the Heart for Educators*

PART 1: Based on the definition of Courage, ask each participant to write a potential headline for a local newspaper, about an educator or student, who lived out this Habit of the Heart in front of him or her. (5 minutes)

PART 2: Call for volunteers to share their headlines, the corresponding story and what it meant to them to see this habit lived out. (10 minutes)

● *Benchmarking Courage*

Time: 1 minute
Materials: Handout 3:1 (Clifton L. Taulbert's Benchmark Chart), multicolored pens/pencils

Have participants get out the Benchmark Chart (Handout 3:1) and, using a different-color writing utensil than their pre-assessment, re-assess their position within Courage after today's learning session and place their new position on the chart.

Journal Writing Prompts

Create a plan that will bring Courage into your classroom on a daily basis and write it out. Implement this plan and record the responses over an extended period of time.

Practical Application

Have participants pull out Handout 10:2, *Personal Strategies to Implement—Courage,* and write one ACTION SPECIFIC strategy, in the top box, that will assist them to start building Courage in their classroom on a daily basis, for all students to benefit from.

Close the session by challenging participants to build Courage among their peers, neighbors and most of all students, on a daily basis. Some great options to start building Friendship can be found on page 104 of Clifton L. Taulbert's *Eight Habits of the Heart for Educators,* under Opportunity to Promote Courage in Your School.

Chapter 11. Hope: The Eighth Habit of the Heart

Summary

Hope—believing in tomorrow, going beyond what we see because we have learned to see with our hearts—summarizes the Eight Habits of the Heart in one word. Who we see these students to be will make all the difference in the world in how we act toward them and for them. As we see tomorrow's citizen-trustee we recognize the need for the previous seven Habits of the Heart. In this chapter, we will look at Hope more closely, to better understand why we each must become this Habit for the continued success of each and every student we encounter.

Discussion Questions

1. Do you know the parents of your students?
2. Have you expressed your Hope for the students to each of their parents?
3. Why is it important to view each student as tomorrow's citizen-trustee? And what role does Hope play in making that vision a reality?

Activities

● *Understanding Hope*

Time: 20 minutes
Materials: Handout 11:1—Hope Activity and Notes Sheet

PART 1: Have each participant read From the Front Porch on page 109 and 110 of Clifton L. Taulbert's *Eight Habits of the Heart for Educators.* (3 minutes)
PART 2: Ask participants how can this Habit of the Heart guide your daily lesson planning and personal expectations of each student you encounter? Have them write a statement of response and then stand and share their responses with another member of the learning group. (12 minutes)

PART 3: While still standing, call for a few volunteers to share their statements. (5 minutes)

● *Benchmarking Hope*

Time: 1 minute
Materials: Handout 3:1 (Clifton L. Taulbert's Benchmark Chart), multicolored pens/pencils

Have participants get out the Benchmark Chart (Handout 3:1) and, using a different-color writing utensil than their pre-assessment, re-assess their position within Hope after today's learning session and place their new position on the chart.

Journal Writing Prompts

After reading the chapter on Hope in Clifton L. Taulbert's book *Eight Habits of the Heart for Educators,* respond to these questions: How can you stick a hopeful foot in the door? What do you expect to happen when you do?

Practical Application

Have participants pull out Handout 11:2, *Personal Strategies to Implement—Hope,* and write one ACTION SPECIFIC strategy, in the top box; they will direct toward a student and one toward a school staff member (bus driver, janitor, etc.) in the presence of students, within 24 hours, that will bring Hope to life.

Close the session by challenging participants to build Hope among their peers, neighbors and most of all students, on a daily basis. Some great options to start building Hope can be found on page 116 of Clifton L. Taulbert's *Eight Habits of the Heart for Educators,* under Opportunity to Promote Hope in Your School.

Chapter 12. Building Community: Sustaining the Excellence

Summary

The significance of daily unselfish acts . . . personal Intentional Unselfishness, has been a common theme among all the chapters of this book and study guide. Remember, for students to be successful, the proper learning environment must exist. This climate can be created by the participants' daily practice of each of the Eight Habits of the Heart. This final chapter, Building Community: Sustaining the Excellence, summarizes the learning that has taken place, supports the importance of each individual educator adopting the Eight Habits of the Heart and introduces you to the result; "a Great Wall of Defense against the tyranny of ignorance."

Discussion Question

1. Do the Eight Habits of the Heart hold an important position within your daily educational routine?

Activity

● *Planning to Sustain the Learning*

Time: 10 minutes
Materials: Handout 12:1—Sustaining the Learning Activity and Notes Sheet

Have participants develop an outline for a lesson plan that will bring to life the Habit of the Heart that has the most room for growth on their Benchmark Chart. (10 minutes)

Journal Writing Prompts

Write down as many ideas on places these Habits can be brought in to how you could bring them to the table and why you want to do so. Allow room after each item for response notes.

Practical Application

Remind participants that there are many additional thought-provoking questions, ideas, comments, and suggestions throughout Clifton L. Taulbert's book, *Eight Habits of the Heart for Educators.*

Close the session by challenging participants to build these Eight Habits of the Heart into daily lesson plans and personal living. Encourage participants to regularly review their notes, writing prompts, personal strategies, and resource text to ensure that they continue to see tomorrow's citizen-trustee in today's youth.

Resources for Extending Your Learning

Closing the Achievement Gap, featuring Glenn Singleton

> Introduces the Four Agreements and Six Conditions of Courageous Conversation. Also features classrooms, schools, and districts that have used Courageous Conversations to begin closing their racial achievement gaps.
> *(The Video Journal of Education.)*

Culturally Proficient Instruction (Multimedia Kit), featuring Kikanza Nuri Robins, Randall B. Lindsey, Delores Lindsey, and Raymond D. Terrell (Corwin Press, 2007)

> Cultural proficiency enables educators to create an inclusive and instructionally powerful learning environment. It encompasses five essential elements: assessing culture, valuing diversity, managing the dynamics of difference, adapting to diversity, and institutionalizing cultural knowledge. Providing agendas, overheads, handouts, and workshop activities, this powerful multimedia training gives staff developers the tools to create high-quality professional learning—from a one-day workshop to a year-long study group.

No Excuses! How to Increase Minority Student Achievement, including Beverly Daniel Tatum, Kati Haycock, James Comer, Sonia Nieto, Gary Howard, Jamie Almanzan, Bonnie Davis, and other experts

> Features diverse secondary and elementary schools from across the United States who have closed their racial achievement gaps. Based on the work of these schools, the Equity Framework is a model that shows how educators can begin to address

23

achievement inequities by focusing on Leadership, School Culture, and Teaching and Learning.
(*The Video Journal of Education/School Improvement Network.*)

Using Data to Close the Achievement Gap, featuring Ruth Johnson

Learn how to use data to change the academic culture of schools, with an emphasis on equity and access for all students. Features schools that successfully use quantitative and qualitative data on a daily basis to guide student learning. (*The Video Journal of Education/School Improvement Network.*)

Professional Development Books

The Right to Learn, by Linda Darling-Hammond
> Published by Jossey-Bass, 1997.

How to Teach Students Who Don't Look Like You, by Bonnie Davis
> Published by Corwin Press, 2006.

Using Data to Close the Achievement Gap, by Ruth Johnson
> Published by Corwin Press, 2002.

Cultural Proficiency: A Manual for School Leaders (**Second Edition**), by Randall B. Lindsey, Kikanza Nuri Robins, and Raymond D. Terrell
> Published by Corwin Press, 2003.

"Why Are All the Black Kids Sitting Together in the Cafeteria?" and Other Conversations About Race, by Beverly Daniel Tatum
> Published by HarperCollins, 1997.

Race Matters, by Cornel West
> Published by Beacon Press, 2001.

Handouts

Handout 1:1. One Powerful Word

Notes

Handout 3:1. Clifton L. Taulbert's Benchmark Chart

P E R S O N A L   A S S E S S M E N T

	1	2	3	4	5	6	7	8
Nurturing Attitude	●	○	○	○	○	○	○	○
Responsibility	●	○	○	○	○	○	○	○
Dependability	●	○	○	○	○	○	○	○
Friendship	●	○	○	○	○	○	○	○
Brotherhood	●	○	○	○	○	○	○	○
High Expectations	●	○	○	○	○	○	○	○
Courage	●	○	○	○	○	○	○	○
Hope	●	○	○	○	○	○	○	○

Apprentice   Journeyman   Skilled

Based upon your understanding of the **Eight Habits of the Heart,** please indicate your position.

NOTE: We all start on the "Apprentice" level!

NAME: _____   DATE: _____

The Building Community Institute

Handout 4:1. Nurturing Attitude Activity and Notes

Unselfish Deeds and Acts

MY POWERFUL CHARACTERISTIC

Notes

Handout 4:2. Personal Strategy to Implement—Nurturing Attitude

To build Nurturing Attitude within the presence of a Student in the next 24 hours, I will . . .

Response/Reaction to Strategy Implementation

Handout 5:1. Responsibility Activity and Notes

My Personal Representative:

_____

The Impact

Notes

Handout 5:2. Personal Strategy to Implement—Responsibility

To bring Responsibility to life for my students, in the next 24 hours, I will . . .

Response/Reaction to Strategy Implementation

Handout 6:1. Dependability Activity and Notes

Should Look Like

Looks Like

Notes

Handout: 6.2. Personal Strategy to Implement—Dependability

To bring Dependability to life for my students, in the next 24 hours, I will . . .

To bring Dependability to life for parents, in the next 24 hours, I will . . .

Response/Reaction to Strategy Implementation

Handout 7:1. Friendship Activity and Notes

Impacting Students

Impacting Parents/Caretakers

Impacting Educators

Notes

Handout 7:2. "Blind Berta" Excerpt

I also saw friendship practiced each time Blind Berta came to town. She always ended up staying with Miss Shugg Payne, who lived down below the colored school, but somehow everyone seemed to be on notice that she was coming to stay a spell. She had no Seeing Eye dog, only a crooked cane that always tapped along in front of her, but it didn't matter. The entire colored community had special stops along the way to accommodate their friend. Her visits gave them a chance to show their affection. The best food would be cooked, the meat finely chopped, and Blind Berta would be carefully situated on each front porch, eating, laughing, and talking—just as all friends do. I don't know where this lady called home, but every year she would appear, regular as clockwork. For the longest time I thought "Blind Berta" was her name, not a description of her lot in life. If she ever felt lost or alone, her laughter never let on, and the people's friendship seemed to be her vision.

Handout 7:3. Personal Strategy to Implement—Friendship

To bring Friendship to life for my students, in the next 24 hours, I will . . .

_____

To bring Friendship to life in front of my students, in the next 24 hours, I will . . .

Response/Reaction to Strategy Implementation

Handout 8:1. Brotherhood Activity and Notes

The Look of Brotherhood

Notes

Handout 8:2. Personal Strategy to Implement—Brotherhood

To reach beyond comfortable and build Brotherhood, in front of my students within the next 24 hours, I will . . .

Response/Reaction to Strategy Implementation

Handout 9:1. High Expectations Activity and Notes

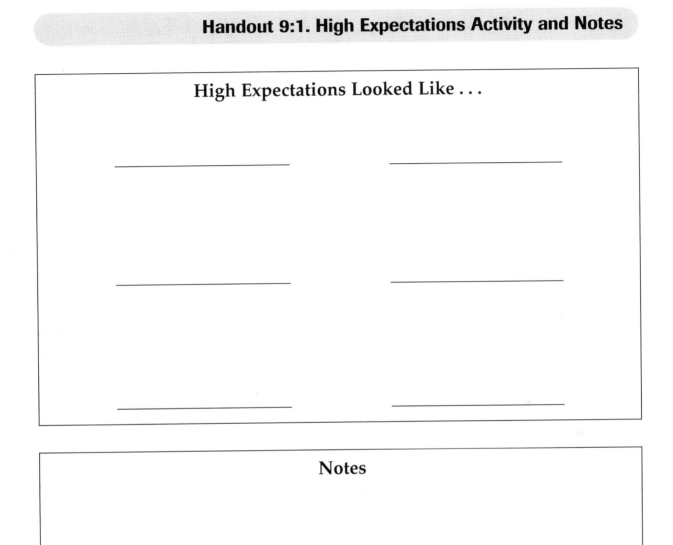

High Expectations Looked Like . . .

Notes

Handout 9:2. Personal Strategy to Implement—High Expectations

To bring High Expectations to life, in front of my students, within the next 24 hours, I will . . .

Response/Reaction to Strategy Implementation

Handout 10:1. Courage Activity and Notes

This Just In . . .

Notes

Handout 10:2. Personal Strategy to Implement—Courage

To start building Courage within the next 24 hours, in my classroom, I will . . .

Response/Reaction to Strategy Implementation

Handout 11:1. Hope Activity and Notes

Hope Can Guide Me Through . . .

Notes

Handout 11:2. Personal Strategy to Implement—Hope

To bring Hope to life for my students, in the next 24 hours, I will . . .

To bring Hope to life in front of my students, in the next 24 hours, I will . . .

Response/Reaction to Strategy Implementation

Handout 12:1. Sustaining the Learning Activity and Notes

My Lesson Plan Outline:

Sample Workshop Agendas

Welcome & Introduction (5 minutes)
- Read the Chapter 1 summary and handle all logistical details of the day

Chapter 1. Building Community . . . The Foundation for Excellence (30 minutes)
- Discuss one opening question, Community Activity, Journal and Strategy

Chapter 2. Building Community . . . The Human Touch (20 minutes)
- Choose two questions for discussion, Postcard Activity, Journal and Strategy

Chapter 3. Building Community . . . Life Lessons From the Mississippi Delta (10 minutes)
- Discussion Questions, Benchmark Activity

Break (12 minutes)

Chapter 4. Nurturing Attitude: The First Habit of the Heart (12 minutes)
- Reading, Group Discussion, Benchmark, Strategy

Chapter 5. Responsibility: The Second Habit of the Heart (15 minutes)
- Reading, Group Discussion, Benchmark, Strategy

Chapter 6. Dependability: The Third Habit of the Heart (15 minutes)
- One discussion question, Group Discussion Activity, Benchmark, Strategy

Chapter 7. Friendship: The Fourth Habit of the Heart
(20 minutes)

- Two discussion questions, Activity Questions #1 & #2, Benchmark, Strategy

Chapter 8. Brotherhood: The Fifth Habit of the Heart
(20 minutes)

- Summary Reading, Discussion Questions, Benchmark, Strategy

Chapter 9. High Expectations: The Sixth Habit of the Heart
(25 minutes)

- One discussion question, Activity Discussion, Journal Writing, Benchmark, Strategy

Chapter 10. Courage: The Seventh Habit of the Heart
(20 minutes)

- Discussion Questions #1 and #4, Activity, Benchmark, Strategy

Chapter 11. Hope: The Eighth Habit of the Heart (20 minutes)

- Discussion Questions #1 and #3, Lesson Plan Outline, Benchmark, Strategy

Chapter 12. Building Community: Sustaining the Excellence
(10 minutes)

- Summary Reading, Activity, Wrap-up

One-Day Workshop Agenda

Welcome & Introduction (10 minutes)
- Read the Chapter 1 summary, all logistical details of the day

Chapter 1. Building Community . . . The Foundation for Excellence (40 minutes)

- Discuss three opening questions, Community Activity, Journal, Strategy

Chapter 2. Building Community . . . The Human Touch
(40 minutes)

- Choose two questions for discussion, Postcard Activity, Journal, Strategy

Chapter 3. Building Community . . . Life Lessons from the Mississippi Delta (40 minutes)

- Summary Reading, Two Discussion Questions, Benchmark Activity, Journal, Strategy

Break (12 minutes)

Chapter 4. Nurturing Attitude: The First Habit of the Heart (45 minutes)

- Summary Reading, One Discussion Question, Activity, Benchmark, Journal, Strategy

Chapter 5. Responsibility: The Second Habit of the Heart (30 minutes)

- Reading, One Discussion Question, Activity, Benchmark, Journal, Strategy

Lunch (55 minutes)

Chapter 6. Dependability: The Third Habit of the Heart (35 minutes)

- Definition reading, One Discussion Question, Activity, Benchmark, Journal, Strategy

Chapter 7. Friendship: The Fourth Habit of the Heart (30 Minutes)

- Friendship Definition, Two Discussion Questions, Activity, Benchmark, Strategy

Break (7 minutes)

Chapter 8. Brotherhood: The Fifth Habit of the Heart (30 minutes)

- Summary Reading, One Discussion Question, Benchmark, Strategy

Chapter 9. High Expectations: The Sixth Habit of the Heart (25 minutes)

- Summary reading, Two Discussion Questions, Activity, Benchmark, Journal, Strategy

Chapter 10. Courage: The Seventh Habit of the Heart (35 minutes)

- Summary reading, Two Discussion Questions, Activity, Benchmark, Journal, Strategy

Chapter 11. Hope: The Eighth Habit of the Heart (25 minutes)

- Definition reading, Two Discussion Questions, Activity, Benchmark, Strategy

Chapter 12. Building Community: Sustaining the Excellence (20 minutes)

- Summary Reading, Activity, Wrap-up

Workshop Evaluation Form

- How well did the seminar meet the goals and objectives?

- How will you apply what you learned during this seminar in your daily professional life?

- What professional support will you need to implement what you have learned from this seminar?

- How well did the topics explored in this seminar meet a specific need in your school or district?

- How relevant was this topic to your professional life?

Process

- How well did the instructional techniques and activities facilitate your understanding of the topic?

- How can you incorporate the activities learned today into your daily professional life?

- Were a variety of learning experiences included in the seminar?

- Was any particular activity memorable? What made it stand out?

Context

- Were the facilities conducive to learning?

- Were the accommodations adequate for the activities involved?

Overall

- Overall, how successful would you consider this seminar? Please include a brief comment or explanation.

- What was the most valuable thing you gained from this seminar experience?

Additional Comments

Source: Adapted from *Evaluating Professional Development* by Thomas R. Guskey, Corwin Press. 2000.

Notes

CORWIN PRESS

The Corwin Press logo—a raven striding across an open book—represents the union of courage and learning. Corwin Press is committed to improving education for all learners by publishing books and other professional development resources for those serving the field of PreK–12 education. By providing practical, hands-on materials, Corwin Press continues to carry out the promise of its motto: **"Helping Educators Do Their Work Better."**

Printed in the United States
By Bookmasters